For Alan Dayton

with Best Wishes

Markéta Zvelebil

GW00708204

WAVES AGAINST A SHORE

MARKÉTA ZVELEBIL

MINERVA PRESS
MONTREUX LONDON WASHINGTON

WAVES AGAINST A SHORE

For my parents,
and with thanks to all my friends.

I am soaring
        high.
And even higher
        will I go.
I am filled with
        longing
and
        tantalising joy.

I am diving
        deep
And even deeper
        will I search
For words
        with which
I am writing
        drawing
Painting thoughts
        on
           a
                page.

WORDS

Loyalty,
I long for
but it is a
dead word
in a world
going dead.

Compassion,
I seek for
but it is a
lost word
in a world
losing itself.

Honour,
I ask for
but it is a
scorned word
in a world
scorning her own existence

Freedom
I beg for
but it is a
misused word
in a world
being misused.

Death
I wait for
but it is a
forbidden word
in a world
that forbids all but death.

WINTER

My mind is
    blank.
        Empty of all
            thoughts
                ideas
                    reflections and
                        ideals.

My heart is
    hollow.
        Empty of all
            feelings
                emotions
                  anger
                    love or
                      hate.

My body is
    barren.
        Empty of all
            energy
                movement
                  strength and
                    will.

My soul is
    dead.
        Empty of all
            longing
                desire
                  seeking
                    expectation and
                      HOPE

WAR

Midnight has just sounded
The church bells have rung.
Silence from the wounded
the warm summer night has wrung.

Bodies piled upon one an other
'tis the sad fact of war
this man to man slaughter
'tis a beast, 'tis a whore

Broken bodies all around
broken bones sticking out
dead men, once human, abound
there is nothing left, nought.

A solitary dove does fly
looks down upon the human carnage
a tear in its eye, but it does not cry
there is nothing left to salvage.

When will people learn
that useless waste of war

HIS TOUCH

The tingling of
                    his Touch
his fingers moving
            from my shoulders
                    to that certain place
                            along the nape
                                    of
                    my neck

A tender caress.
Warmth seeps through
                    the Touch
of his hands.
Cupping my face,
            guiding it closer
                    nearer to his.

His finger-tips
            explore my cheeks
            with his Touch
as closer and closer
            his lips
are brought
            to my
                    lips

        We touch.

'Tis night

there is the light

of my star

of so near, yet so far.

SOLDIERS

Tiny fists,

        I am tough

Take arms

        little ones

Tiny hands

        hold big gun

Take aim

        grow up

Treasured one

        shoot!

Tough now

                he

        stares at

Tiny bodies

        at his

                feet.

Let me sleep
Let me be
        unborn, in safety
protected
        never neglected
In this world of insanity

Never to be hurt
        physically or mentally
in a life so absurd
        waiting to reach senility

Let me sleep
Let me be
Let me not begin
Just so that I can end
        Let me not live
        So that I cannot die.

THE SEA

Blue
  so dark yet so clear
                lucid
glassy
  reflecting refracting light
             bright sunshine

Blue
  so deep
           dark and dense restless
           constantly moving
  the mobility of your body
         is immense
         frightening yet reassuring

Oh sea
sheer voluminous power
         of never-ending eternal life.

TO CHILDREN OF RWANDA

Large eyes,
  black eyes,
  stare
      not understanding
      not comprehending.

WHY?
  WHY does it want
        to harm me?
        to kill me?
          To take away
  my barely began
                life?

Small legs,
  strong legs
          carry
          the large eyes.
    with no thought
    following
    being led
by all the other
    frightened
    bewildered
Large eyes.

Large eyes
      closed
      at last
            the peace
            they sought
      is found

Large eyes
      now rest
      in a child's head
hacked off –
      by a machete
            possessed
            with all the
      World's Madness.

Another life
            lost
            left
      on the never-ending
dirt-track.

21 AUGUST 1968

For all the beauty in the world
      for all the reaches in its hold
Not a finer thing is found
      than freedom, to fly and not be bound.

But this treasure is easily destroyed or lost
      to some country's self-appointed host.
And so he says; your country is my guest
      therefore you can forgo and forget the
rest.

And as a gift he sends
      big, grinding whining tanks.
Just to keep an eye
      that there is nothing you can try.

And as people cry, go away, go home leave us alone
      the tanks grind on and on, on the old
      cobblestones.
And so it happened in Prague one night
      leaving the city in shadows, not a flicker
      of light
That could bring a speck of hope
      to cut the binding rope.

OPPOSITE SIDES

He holds
     his child
in his arms.
Cradling it
     filled with
     Love
     Pride and
          Joy

He holds
     his gun
in his arms
Cradling it
     filled with   He does not
     Love   really know
     Pride and   the reason
          Hate   his heart
                    and
                       soul
are filled
     with
          rage.
But within him
his hate
     is
burning,
     churning
     and
          swelling.
It feeds
     on
          lies
laced with truth.
It satisfies
     its hunger
with his gun.

He holds
        his gun
in his arms.
Poised,
        ready
                to aim
One single
        shot
Darkens the
        sun.

Hate abated
He takes
        his child
from the cot.
Cradling it
        soothingly
in his arms.

                A father holds
                        his child
                in his arms.
                Cradling it
                        filled with
                        grief
                                pain and
                                    sorrow.

                Hot

                blood
                freely runs
                from
                one single
                        shot.

THE MURDER

Footsteps
           approaching
nearer and nearer
           step by step
the heart is beating
waiting for the bearer
of the all ending death.
Wind howls, dog howls
a cry is lost to the universe.
Silence, not a soul
in sight.
The life that was hers
is lost in the night.
Footsteps
           fade
further and further
           step by step.

9 O'CLOCK NEWS

My mind is drifting
    unfocused
        like a dry
    splint of wood
        on
    the eternally
    silent sea

My mind is unconnected
    withdrawn
        from reality
    like a lover's whisper
        on
    a windy morning

My mind is torn
    tortured
        by fear and emotions
    like the everlasting
        screams
    of those burned in
    eternal hell

My mind is saddened
    for the unceasing
        violence
    weeping
        like a mother
    for her lost child

My mind
    My heart
        My soul

IN MEMORY: 50 YEARS AFTER THE HOLOCAUST

Step
       by
           Step

Each step
     takes me
         nearer to my
             death.

She awaits me
     welcomes me
         with her
             Zyklone-B-laced
                breath.

Her arms
     grip me
         tighter
            and tighter.
Breaking
     bone by
         brittle bone
            in my chest.

As I fight
     for my last
         gasp
             of
               breath

Her hateful howl
     loudly echoes
          through my ears.

As torturously
     last words
          I force
               through my lips.

Through tears
     I whisper
          "Shema…"
               before
                    death.

FOR LEONARD NIMOY

A Drop
 I catch
  and hold
I open
 My hand
 and
   a drop of
      Blood
        green as emerald
I hold
 in
  my hand

His eyes
 dark and deep
      sombre
 filled with
      compassion
       wisdom
          look
Silent stare
      at me
       staring at
         The drop of blood
          emerald green
          in the palm
           of my hand.

Blood
    not red
      but
        green.
Alien
    yet so
      familiar.
All my hopes
    dreams
      expectations
          revealed
            in one
              single drop.

A cut
    and
      I mix
        the red
            with
        the green
      unifying
      the life
of all the Universe.

Pure joy
  fills my soul
        immense
overwhelming
        joy
        as I watch
        the drop of
            emerald

I close my hand
  and hold
        that
        Jewel

Life
> a path to acceptance
> a one-way road.

Life

> a path to learn
>   to accept
> the one-way road

Life

> the beginning
>   of the end
> of the one-way road.

Life

> the way
>   to peacefully reach
> the end of the one-way road.

Life

> a short lease
>   of a body
> to travel the one-way road.

HYPERSPACE

I am a

   particle.

I am a

   wave.

I am

   matter.

I am

   Energy.

I am

   All

I am

   nothing.

I am

   I

I am

   not!

HUNGER
For all the starving children in the world

Little bird eat
as much as you need
for not long shall you live
as more I will not give
and while you starve
I will laugh
For I am of the human race
the animal with the two fold face
one is good hearted but that one has departed
the evil stays behind
conquering my mind.

HOPE

Wall
confinement
           enclosed inside
imprisoned
           is my soul
in this imperfect body
shell of flesh and blood
pain suffering
           aching agony
the body endures
           the soul trapped
stays immobile
           unmoving
batting its wings
           waiting, hoping
               praying for freeing flight
                  for death.

TO THE HOMELESS OF LONDON

Monday morning
   The sun is shining.
         Sun's rays drawing
            intricate patterns
               in rain's puddles
               on the pavement
           He sits.
        Blanket neatly folded
  watching passers-by.
  A few stop
      to drop
         a penny or two
  into his lap.

Tuesday morning
  White clouds forming
      delicate sculptures
        reflected
          in rain's puddles
          on the pavement
       He sits.
     Blanket wrapped
 around the still form
 Eyes dull
 In his hand
    a can
 watching
    not seeing
    the passers-by
 frowning at him.

Wednesday morning
    Grey sky
        shadowless creations
           of the world
              reflected
                on the pavement
              He sits.
            Slouching against
        the wall.
    An empty can
    or two
    by his side.
    Empty eyes
        stare
           at passers-by
           who turn their
        face and hearts
away.

Thursday morning
    Icy wind blowing
        leaves chasing changing
           forms
              on the pavement
        He sits.
    Frozen
        still
            against the wall.
    No cans in
        evidence
    Dead eyes
        accusing
            the passers-by
        who
    pretended
    he is not there.

Friday morning
    Sun is peeking out
        sharp shadows
            play with composition
            on the pavement
        Empty now.
    No eyes
        left
            to watch the
        relieved
    passers-by.

FRIENDSHIP

I walk and I dream
holding your hand
my thoughts are free
to float downstream
they pass from farmland
to forest and mountains.
They float and are free
I walk and I speak
I tell you my hopes
my dreams and desires.
They are all yours to keep
they are my binding ropes
my dreams and my hopes

DAY BY DAY

In the morning

    I ask why.

At noon

    I try

        to understand

In the evening

    I cry

At night,

    I wish to die

        for I still do not understand.

COLOURS

I wear only
      white.

White reflects
      like a mirror

My deepest self
      my emotions
stay hidden
behind the reflections
      of the mirror.

I wear only
      black
Black absorbs
      the shocks and horrors
          the love and joys
              of life.

They are within to stay
      and not a ray
         will be let
            out.

I.

Who am I
Why am I
Where am I
When am I
What am I
      am I a circle of conflicting
           thoughts and
                  emotions
                            with no beginning
                  and no end
              unanswered
        circular string of futile life?
I am thought
I am thine
I am there
I am then
I am that.

BIRTH

Blank page
You open yourself to me
Like a petal on a rose
A new leaf on a tree
Waiting –
for what?
A few words of wisdom
A poem a piece of prose a song?
To put down on paper
Emotions so strong
They couldn't wait
Having waited for so long
They burst forth

Black on white
The ink shimmering on
White light

Blank page
No longer blank
Despoiled
Used
Innocence lost

Life at any cost!